STORM TOWARD MORNING

MALACHI BLACK
STORM TOWARD MORNING

COPPER CANYON PRESS
PORT TOWNSEND, WASHINGTON

Cover art: Louis le Brocquy, *Head with Open Mouth*, 1971. Oil on canvas, 46 x 38 cm. © Estate of Louis le Brocquy

Copper Canyon Press is in residence at Fort Worden State Park in Port Townsend, Washington, under the auspices of Centrum. Centrum is a gathering place for artists and creative thinkers from around the world, students of all ages and backgrounds, and audiences seeking extraordinary cultural enrichment.

LIBRARY OF CONGRESS CATALOGING-IN-PUBLICATION DATA

Black, Malachi.
  [Poems. Selections]
  Storm toward morning / Malachi Black.
    pages cm

  ISBN 978-1-55659-472-4 (paperback)
  I. Title.

PS3602.L32A6 2014
811'.6—dc23

                2014015610

          98765432 FIRST PRINTING

COPPER CANYON PRESS
Post Office Box 271
Port Townsend, Washington 98368
www.coppercanyonpress.org

to MSM

CONTENTS

I

I shall fall
Like a bright exhalation in the evening,
And no man see me more.

Henry VIII, 3.2.225–27

STORM TOWARD MORNING

I

Under an Eclipsing Moon

I am the black strokes on the baby grand
piano in whose hands I am tonight

beside the hospital, a yellow gram
of Valium with me in the bright

side of this house behind a darkened high
school baseball diamond. Here it's too dim,

too overcast to know what sort of slim
lip the moon has grooved into the sky.

So what can I, whose veins are purpled through
with bits of broken glass and vodka,

whose heart claps like a shoe, what can I do
but play a drunken, pill-induced sonata,

watch it backflip and rebound, caterwauling
in a somersault of sound around the room?

Traveling by Train

And faster past another frozen river,
the brambles, shrubs, and underbrush of dead
woods and the garbage that was left behind
by runaways and skunks: the plastic bags
and twine, shoes beside forgotten brands
of beer whose cans, so battered by the weather,
have all but disappeared—like the whiteness
of a smoke after it's cleared. And you've been on
this train too long to know the time: you're lost
between the meter and the desperate rhyme
of clacking tracks. Home is nothing here.
You're gone and in the going; can't come back.

Insomnia & So On

Fat bed, lick the black cat in my mouth
each morning. Unfasten all the bones

that make a head, and let me rest: unknown
among the oboe-throated geese gone south

to drop their down and sleep beside the out-
bound tides. Now there's no nighttime I can own

that isn't anxious as a phone
about to ring. Give me some doubt

on loan; give me a way to get away
from what I know. I pace until the sun

is in my window. I lie down. I'm a coal:
I smolder to a bloodshot glow. Each day

I die down in my bed of snow, undone
by my red mind and what it woke.

Coming & Going

All day long I plunge into the ether
like a tongue into a fragile glass

of water. Thirsty for an urgency
to squint in the crouched sun, to turn

the doorknob of a corner, to open
up into an avenue and run,

I clop unevenly along the sidewalks,
crooked and vaguely caving in,

like some demented, avid mailman.
Though I know no one is expecting me,

worrying a wristwatch, pacing
and awaiting and awaiting

my delivery, I stroll just the same:
there must be something in the air to blame.

To the Moon

Once you were a bubble on the surface
of a puddle made of rain. Once you were

the bottom of a birthday hat. Once
you were the forehead of a newborn,

boring and forlorn. Once you were
and so you anciently remain: turning away

from me a little more each day. I say
your name. I say what others say. I

only have one word for you. Today
you're already awake and it's today.

You're already awake. Are you in love
with me? What and whom exactly do you see

when I am weary-eyed but wired, crookedly
looking up to you as you look down on me?

Sifting in the Afternoon

Some people might describe this room as spare:
a bedside table and an ashtray and an antique

chair; a mattress and a coffee mug;
an unwashed cotton blanket and a rug

my mother used to own. I used to have
a phone. I used to have another

room, a bigger broom, a wetter sponge.
I used to water my bouquet

of paperclips and empty pens, of things
I thought I'd want to say if given chance;

but now, to live, to sit somehow, to watch
a particle of thought dote on the dust

and dwindle in a little grid of shadow
on the sunset's patchy rust seems just enough.

Ode to the Sun

You repeat yourself like no one
I know. Steadily somewhere,
you roll unnoticeably forward

even now, showing. Your finger
lifts the flowers and their faces
by the chin, but you will leave them

behind like blown-out beach
umbrellas. You will always reach
and extend. You will always

try to keep me to yourself on Monday
mornings: You will glare and I will go,
but you don't care and you can't know.

I will look at you too long and cry.
I will wonder where you've gone, at night.
I'll fall asleep and dream: an acorn.

You are nothing but a breast, round
behind a blouse of clouds built to be
unbuttoned. You love: You share

yourself and you are always naked:
You love: You show us how to take
our places: You love: You cover our faces

This Gentle Surgery

Once more the bright blade of a morning breeze
glides almost too easily through me,

and from the scuffle I've been sutured to
some flap of me is freed: I am severed

like a simile: an honest tenor
trembling toward the vehicle I mean

to be: a blackbird licking half-notes
from the muscled, sap-damp branches

of the sugar maple tree... though I am still
a part of any part of every particle

of me, though I'll be softly reconstructed
by the white gloves of metonymy,

I grieve: there is no feeling in a cut
that doesn't heal a bit too much.

Psalm: Pater Noster

I am your plum:
                    Enfold me
in the shadow of your mouth
and I will echo as a taste
against your tongue:
                    I am
your praise: I am
the breath bent by your phrase: I am
the string plucked for your song: I am

your son: Another vein
built for the humming of your blood

Drifting at Midday

Now I can see: even the trees
are tired: they are bones bent forward

in a skin of wind, leaning in
osteoporosis, reaching

for a little more than any
oxygen can give: when living

is in season, they can live;
but living is no reason

to continue: everything begins:
and everything is desperate

to extend: and everything is
insufficient in the end:

and everything is ending:
Now I can see: even the trees

You

Fool. You used to think a blushing arm that bent
round you in bed, that would extend to you

across a room still crowded with the breath
of friends and pet the dizzy hair above

your party talk–drunk head, could help defend
or even wave away the tiny mess

of rainclouds and the odd, slush-stained galoshes
from the snow globe in your chest. But you

were being young then. Tonight, you brush
the crumbs of birthday cake away from where

you baked it and it sat. Tonight, you get
undressed, and read a bit in bed, and stretch

out into emptiness. You have nothing
to remember. You have no one to forget.

The Beekeeper's Diary

A swarm will surge and stagger from the hive—
a spray of gold aluminum each spring.
Some colonies must break to stay alive,
make way for bodies that a winter brings.
Like any matriarchs, old queens contrive
to feed and keep the weather from new wings.
And so the swarm will drone its discontent:
an orchestra tuning its instruments.

* * *

The bee embodies its pure paradox
fiercely and unself-consciously in turn:
a venom cartridge and a honey stock,
it trembles between sweetness and the burn
of its own thorn. Queen sips the hollyhock's
thin nectar, and then weightlessly returns
to the brood nest. I wonder if she can
taste the venom tipping in her glands.

Rain

again, and on a day
you meant to spend

in other ways than tracing
veins of it descend

the dusty plate glass
of a window by the bed.

Try to make a friend
of anything you can

that's kind enough to give
back what you lend

to its reflection;
tomorrow you will

lose yourself again.

When I Lie Down

to Sleep

I'll count backward from a thousand
till my teeth begin to grind, down

to zero, where the digits tilt and swivel
in a ring around the racing eye

of the tornado I'm made of tonight.
Left alive, I am an opening

too wide, much too much gaping sky
to slip behind the throbbing canopy

of hide I call an eyelid. So let your crow
land in my lashes; close my eyes.

I'll be your nest, a place to rest
built out of syllables of lullabies:

Come to me. Don't go. We have nothing left
to say to one another but hello.

Awake

But who can bear the awful opening
of eyes: the wake-up and its awkward lapse

into anatomy; the gray awareness
of the hips, of tongue on teeth, of spine,

of lips and kneecaps, ears and groin?
I hate the clockwork of the waking mind:

the time trying to break itself in two:
the who I am and who are you, the who

I know and who I knew. As daylight
sprains its way into the room, I know

that sleep is just a matter of degree,
and I'd rather stay awake than mostly be

some feather in a fever dream. So keep
away: take your dead talons out of me.

Sleepwalker, Lost

Who was I when I was a boy? Not small

hands lost among a crush of toys, not

the disk of face I passed when walking by

the window glass, nor the quick pulse

laughing in my chest as I pretended

I knew what it meant to be alive

in cities blitzed and terrified by war...

perhaps I'd been a boy before:

I knew much more then of what

to do than now, smoking a cigarette

and trying to remember how

I wound up sitting in the living

room with one sock on, turned

inside out, and nothing else.

Face to Face

I watch the clock until the teeth
in every gear begin to talk

to me. As if time quivered in an ear,
a nervous tic that I could hear, a meter

pulsing in the vapor of hot voices
in the cold. As if time could be controlled

by silence. As if we could stop the clocks
simply by not talking. We can quarrel

but the time's still told: by pouty lips
formed in wrinkles on the foreheads

of the old men at the bus depot.
We fulfill time's circularity

of logic: our faces are soft dials
turning around a little while.

Mirroring

You must be so tired of my runny eyes,
my muttering and fumbling toward the light

switch at your side, the conversation
that I make when I'm the lonely one

awake and you're the only one who'll take
me in bad shape. It's I you can't escape.

Too many times, I've seen you fake
a lopsided smile. You've seen me break

it with a greeting as I reach to shake
the hand you reach to shake: somehow I

never say goodbye. And maybe I'd admire
you, whose sole machinery is being

what I see when you see me, if only
someone else could be you seeing me.

Against the Glass

Rocking in my midnight robe, I am
alive and in an eye again beside

my kind insomniac, my phantom
glass, companion and my only bride:

this little window giving little shine
to something. What I see I keep

alive. I name the species, I define
the lurch and glimmer, sweep and pry

of eyes against the faint-reflecting glass
by what they can and what I can't

quite grasp: I see a hand, still mine, outstretched
in an attempt to catch the stars that drop

as hailstones in the grass. I see them pass;
these sleepless fingers slip from solid into gas.

Quantum Solstice

If darkness is a dew, then I am made
of moisture: every atom of me

strewn about the backyard as a galaxy
of fixed globes clinging to the bow-bent

blades of grass, each atom bulging
at the belly like a magnifying glass:

I distort what I redress. But dawn
extinguishes the moonbeam, and at last

night shrinks back into shadows,
leaking from the objects that it casts

as independent bodies blinking in
one mass. May I be a black cloud, then,

blooming overhead, wearing daylight
as a dry disguise. Lest you see through

my eyes: two black moons waxed in round blue skies.

As a Draft

Now there is nothing I can touch:
I am an element, an air

of nothing much: a subtle lisp
of what was substance: what was once

a skin and all its fingertips
falling in love with what, with what

it could, with what it was, with what
it could brush up against? I'll clutch

whatever I remember
of the seasons I let skip

across the playgrounds of my blood
and then let go: this is the fall,

and something falling's all I know—
my own old footprints filling up with snow

II

O let me rise
As larks, harmoniously,
And sing this day thy victories:
Then shall the fall further the flight in me.

George Herbert, "Easter Wings (I)"

Quarantine

Lauds

Somehow I am sturdier, more shore
than sea-spray as I thicken through
the bedroom door. I gleam of sickness.
You give me morning, Lord, as you
give earthquake to all architecture.
I can forget.
                     You put that sugar
in the melon's breath, and it is wet
with what you are. (I, too, ferment.)
You rub the hum and simple warmth
of summer from afar into the hips
of insects and of everything.
I can forget.
                     And like the sea,
one more machine without a memory,
I don't believe that you made me.

Prime

I don't believe that you made me
into this tremolo of hands,
this fever, this flat-footed dance
of tendons and the drapery

of skin along a skeleton.
I am that I am: a brittle
ribcage and the hummingbird
of breath that flickers in it.

Incrementally, I stand:
in me are eons and the cramp
of endless ancestry.

Sun is in the leaves again.
I think I see you in the wind
but then I think I see the wind.

Terce

But then I think I see the wind
as an intention, pressing us
with weather. All the pieces
of the air you've put together
somehow know just how to hold
the rain. They somehow know

to funnel and unfold, to swerve
the snow, to rake the beaches
and to slope the arcing seagull's wings.
As wind inside a shell: they know
you in themselves. I'll find you out;
I can know you as a hint in things.

I do. And through the window
I have known you as an opening.

Sext

I have known you as an opening
of curtains as a light blurts through
the sky. But this is afternoon
and afternoon is not the time

to hunt you with the hot globe
of a human eye. So I fluster
like a crooked broom in rounds
within the living room, and try
to lift an ear to you. I try.

I cut myself into a cave for you.
To be a trilling blindness
in the infinite vibration
of your murmuring July,
I cut myself into a cave for you.

None

I cut myself into a cave for you,
but you are quiet. You are shy:

an only child, you still hide
from blame and invitations

and you constantly deny
all suitors. I will not be

defied: *you* are the tongue
I plunge into this begging

razorblade so brightened
by my spiderweb of blood,

you are the one: you are
the venom in the serpent

I have tried not to become,
my Lord. You are the one.

Vespers

My Lord, you are the one:
your breath has blown away
            the visionary sun
and now suffocates the skyline
            with a dusk. If only once,
I wish that you could shudder
with my pulse,   double over
and convulse   on the stitches
in the skin that I slash wishes in.
            But, Lord, you are the gulf
between the hoped-for
                        and the happening:
You've won.   So what is left for me
when what is left for me has come?

Compline

when what is left for me has come:
when what is left has left its wing
in something slumped against a door:
when what is left for me has come
to nothing ever after and before
this kingdom come to nothing:
when what has come is nothing more
than what was left and what was left
is nothing more than what has come
to nothing ever after and before:
if what is left is what is meant
for me and what is meant for me
is nothing come to nothing come
to this kingdom come to nothing:

Nocturne

To This Kingdom Come to Nothing:

I have itemized the night. I have held
within the livid tissue of my mouth
every particle of light and even now
I am a maze of radiation. I have felt
in each of my one hundred trillion cells
the rapturous, proud swell of darkling sounds
whose undulations break a body down
to sprays of elemental matter. As well
I have obtained a straightforward account
of the forces and conditions that propelled
the universe to burst from nothing else
and I can tell of every trembling genesis.

There is no end,

> What Has Come
> > Will Come Again

Vigils

There is no end: what has come will come again
will come again: and then distend: and then
and then: and then again: there is no end

to origin and and: there is again
and born again: there is the forming and:
the midnight curling into morning and

the glory and again: there is no end:
there is the blessing in an and and an again:
the limitlessly yessing of began

begins incessantly again: and then
the infinite undressing of all when
there is the lifting everything again

the glowing endlessness and then
the floating endlessly again

Matins

The floating endlessly again:
the glowing and the growing back
again as I am as I can and I can stand.
I understand.
           Though I am fashioned
in the haggard image of a man,
I am an atom of the aperture.

I am as a nerve inside a gland.

I understand. Though I am fashioned
as I am, I am a perch for the eternal
and a purse for what it lends.
I understand.
           Though flakes of fire
overwhelm the fallen snow, though ice
caps melt, though oceans freeze or overflow,
somehow I am sturdier, more sure.

FINIS.

III

A Memo to the Self-Possessed

Caesar, I can see the blue breath
      of a meteor
rake the naked vacancy of sky:
      an exhalation

aching from the fate of Gemini
      for conflagration
in the hazard of our atmosphere.
      The teeth of Earth

burn with the friction of their gear,
      turning once and then
again as mathematically the year
      painstakingly divides

our tribulations. Here,
      and only here,
the moisture in a sigh is equal
      to both fever bead

and tear; the heart beats
      as an instrument
of sciences unclear to its own
      monitors. Here,

we try but find no foothold
      on an enormous sphere:
we falter as the circus ball revolves
      then disappear

just after our first flatlined
      equilibrium.
And where are you tonight,
      Marcus Aurelius?

Are you as steady as the fulcrum,
      or were you just
another victim of the lever?
      My bony liege,

even heady Archimedes
      was dissevered
by the seared blade of a siege;
      not Aristotle

nor his soft-wrought Golden Mean
      can buttress us
against an iron sword's keen
      cut-and-thrust:

caught in our palpitating selves,
      we are furious
machines. Caesar, I have seen
      the sea in shelves

of foam and I have known it
      as an ancestor.
In this undertow of pulse,
      what solemn stroke

do you propose? What Stoic
      song can cool, can calm
the meteoric note of my hot throat
      as it explodes?

That the Bones Which Thou Hast Broken May Rejoice

Born for the briar
                        Lord
my cheek, rounded as the unripe
                        nectarine but
                                    pliant as a moss grown over mud

Gorge on the salt fruit of the violet
            cord,
                        vein
lacing muscle to its unrepentant
                                    blood

I am the harvest
                        Lord
femur, rib, and clavicle
                        to be hollowed as the flute is
            for a song

Lift up
            my skull, the halved gourd
                                    so the blank
note of the wind
                        can find its form

Query on Typography

What is the light
        inside the opening
of every letter: white
        behind the angles
is a language bright
        because a curvature
of space inside
        a line is visible
is script a sign
        of what it does
or does not occupy
        scripture the covenant
of eye and I
        with word or what
the word defines
        which is source
and which is shrine
        the light of body
or the light behind?

I Have Forgotten You, My Self

But still, like smoke
above a blown-out match

you linger in the dimming
aftermath, grayer and fainter

than a breath: a quiver
silvering the once-gold air,

slowly curling over
but more slowly blurring back

to silhouettes: black
edges in the rainlight

giving shape to aging
furniture. Maybe it's less

that I have failed
to recollect, more that

you've risen undetected
to the vents: a scent

some facet of me left
unused yet intact, removed

but resident: like a clef
on empty sheet music

inside a closed piano bench.

Our Lady of Sorrows

What is it that she wanted? Each bird invisibly
was harnessed like a tent-peg to the tarpaulin
of spring—each sparrow, scarlet tanager, and starling
bartered with the wind-stream wing by wing to haul
across the hemisphere a little portion of the sky
to fit now, fixtured simply, in the wintered planet
of her eye. What is it that she wanted if not spring?—
sprigs broken into crocuses, a butterflying openness
clothing the magnolias with a breeze: a troubling
of the shrubbery, a fraught commotion of the honeybee,
a wrinkling of sunlight through forsythia trees.
All this is hers to hover in, to walk through and be
covered in,—to grieve. All this is sad extravagance,
as only those who are not looking cannot see.

To the Executioner

Your quickness is a kind

of love. As you administer

the incapacitating drugs,

you are the millisecond's

witness. You live

within the distance between

fingertip and glove as if

the absence of a fingerprint

were innocence. Still,

you alone know how

a kill can be redeemed:

Even the dead have dreams.

Morning Shows

The walls watch and no one knows
You're boxing books and won't be home
Alone again when morning shows.

Next door, they tumble under covers. Though
There are lovers like a laundry load,
The walls watch and no one knows

Their names, nor why they won't just go
To sleep... snub nose nestled next to freckled nose.
Alone again when morning shows,

You still think in summer of the snow
And wonder how to package winter's clothes.
The walls watch and no one knows

Your suitcase is too full to close.
Upstairs, some furniture against the floorboards groans.
Alone again when morning shows,

That neighbor greets her love of ghosts—
Thinks rearranging things can bring gone husbands home.
The walls watch and no one knows.

Alone again when morning shows.

Dining after Dawn

Behind this round and solid sound, I square:
an egg is scrambled on the scalding pan

I am; I am what I can't quite withstand.
A flippant wind, disheveling my hair,

is there to cool and oscillate the air
around me when the stove ignites again,

but I am almost liquid. When I can,
I speak through bubbles in the skin that's bare

against the metal. Something I can find
is something lost, is something not to lose,

is something I am song enough to stutter:
if I am just a seed enclosed in rind,

then won't you give me something I can use
when I am walking into water?

The Winter Traveler

Once more the earth is old enough

for snow: a crooked posture of cold

grasses, a white sky sighing down

bare branches, a freeze tightening

each liquid into stone. Tomorrow

and tomorrow and tomorrow

I'll be anchored by a sinking

of my bones into the air

I carry in my clothes, walking

roadside with my wrists exposed

to the horizon. Dear Passerby:

Since I am nothing, I am whole.

I'll be lifted by the wind's edge

and borne home—the day

after the day after tomorrow.

For Love of Ice

I have shivered over sidewalks
        all my life, coughing night
into the hollow of a fist
        that I can't warm,
that I can't seem to steady right
        against cold lips.

I have been windburnt by a trick
        of winter mist, shadow
in the eye that couldn't be
        what I had wished:
some form, some figure in the snow
        to console me.

I have walked for hours underdressed
        to feel frostbite glove
my hands and wrists and I
        have clung to pavement
staring veins into its ice: in love
        with nothing's eyes.

Plainsong

A windshield doesn't care about the sun,
but it will come. And it will smear

across my rearview mirror when it does,
but I'm not done. If I'm unluckily

alive then, I will drive my four-door
suicide past every pleading traffic

sign, through every red light, yellow
line and guardrail clinging to a cliff-side

I can find until my front seat catches
fire from the sparks between my shredded

tires or my engine opens in explosion
I am tired god if you're not

good enough to kill me let me die

Whalesong

A sound strobes through the mood
of murky water. A mouth moves, too,
and bodies almost blue
have brought their barnacles
to burst upon the surface.

* * *

In wind then they are nude.
A crush of sea-spray plumes
before the oxygen can alter:
the breath burns as it soothes
a cloud half in, half out of water.

* * *

With the flicker of a fishtail now
push down: Enter into under
water and the onset of the shudder
buckling the lungs: In sudden
thunder, bones are bent to song—

* * *

Siren: A frightened lightning
strikes the whited eyes and Siren:
Shrieks will rise like steam-heat
swilling in the Siren cries of stillbirth
from a furnace, Siren: Rise

Found

Reeds nibble on the wind.
A face floating in the lake:
Afternoon's first moon.

Growing Season

after the wood of suicides in Dante's Inferno,
Canto XIII

It takes days for the feet to fit through. First the tip of a big toe buds, barely noticeable: a blister on a black branch. But soon the foot is halfway passed, beginning at the arch. Underground, without the sun, it's hard to know how long the ankle takes to bulge, the calf muscle to lump, the knee to shrug down from the branch's broken bark. And there is blood. It dries into an iodine rust over every hard-born inch of skin. The tree can speak, and it will shriek until a whole head hangs by a neck-like stem with a dumb body dangling beneath. And hell has won: once borne, the body drops. Another one's begun.

Metamorphosis

Eat the egg
shell while
you have
a mouth:
in ten days,
little instar,
you will die
without it

Fragments from an Afterlife

I can no longer recall
        the arrowheaded leaves
that suckled on a braid
        of branches, hiding
overripe tangerines.

                *

        Heirloom
tomatoes and a trace
        of blood.

                *

Did tongue ever
        have a memory?

                *

A sudden height
        when something
had occurred to me.

                *

To hurry.
        To be worried.

                *

To have teeth and something
        stuck in them;
to spend every evening

brushing them;
spitting out the paste.

*

The things I used to take
the time to taste.

*

To have eyelids
and be tired.
The weightlessness
of lying
down and not quite dying.

*

A sunburnt face.

*

Fever and the foreignness
it lent
to everything.

*

The paper odor
of the doctor's
office and the cold sting
of the stethoscope.
To have and to hear
a heartbeat

as the pulse rose
        to the ears.

                *

Not just to be a boy,
        but to remember it
much later.
                As in:

Learning how to read
        a wristwatch.
So much puzzlement.

                *

Laughter: how it happened.

                *

Tracing ballpoint etchings
        on a desktop.

                *

Being caught: the feeling
        of fainting
inwardly.

                *

        Time:
a ghost of sunglow

in the eyes
after I looked away.

*

Sometimes we were whispering.

*

There was a way of walking
     in a swimming pool
or stream. There was a way
     of simply walking.
There were streets.

The Puncture

A vein is lightning, forked and full.
Skin dimples like a sail in wind.
Just ease the needle, squeeze, and pull.
It trampolines beneath the tucked-in pin:

Skin dimples like a sail in wind,
A curtsy in the softest skirt.
It trampolines beneath the tucked-in pin,
One worm immersing in its dirt.

A curtsy in the softest skirt;
A winged thing, like a wrinkled gull.
One worm immersing in its dirt.
Heat swarms, encircling one skull.

A winged thing, like a wrinkled gull,
Will sculpt a gust to hug its fringe.
Heat swarms, encircling one skull.
Add water, gunpowder; syringe

Will sculpt a gust to hug its fringe.
Afloat: below the bone, above:
Add water, gunpowder, syringe.
Like waking to the just-dreamed-of.

Afloat: below the bone, above:
When wishes wander from the well.
Like waking to the just-dreamed-of,
The beat slows but repeats itself.

When wishes wander from the well,
And I, I sleep more than I should,
The beat slows but repeats itself:
A slumber pent within the blood.

And I, I sleep more than I should,
Just ease the needle, squeeze, and pull.
A slumber pent within the blood:
A vein is lightning, forked and full.

Prayer for a Slow Death

Let the light be
yellow but not   candlelit, quiet,
                      incandescent,
                                        not cold yet
                                        not quite bright
enough to sting
the eye, close   enough to see
                      beside, clear
                                        enough to read
                                        by, and just near
enough to turn
off morning   after morning,
                      to burn on
                                        absentmindedly
                                        each night

Notes

"Quarantine" is a poem to the possibility of God. Cast as a crown of sonnets in the tradition of John Donne's "La Corona," the ten movements of "Quarantine" derive their logic and arrangement from the Christian monastic prayer cycle known generally as the canonical hours (*horae canonicae*), condensing the traditional quarantine period of forty days and forty nights into the passage of one day. The cycle draws from an assembly of contemporary and historical Catholic, Coptic, and Eastern Orthodox monastic traditions, such that each of the poem's ten prayers corresponds to a different biblical event or religious consideration. The work begins with "Lauds," the Dawn Prayer, which is executed in the "watches" of the night at dawn or predawn, and praises God upon the rising of the sun. It is followed by "Prime," the Early Morning Prayer or First Hour, which commemorates the Creation, the banishment from Eden, and the appearance of Jesus before Caiaphas. "Terce," the Midmorning Prayer or Third Hour, is associated with the descent of the Holy Spirit at Pentecost; "Sext," the Sixth Hour or Midday Prayer, with the Crucifixion; and "None," the Ninth Hour or Midafternoon Prayer, with the death of Jesus. Performed at sunset or upon the lighting of the lamps, "Vespers," the Eleventh Hour or Evening Prayer, is a meditation on the "Light of Christ," while "Compline," the Twelfth Hour or Night Prayer, is a contemplation of death, "our final falling asleep." The Night Hours, variously called "Nocturne," "Vigils," or "Matins," consist of three watches corresponding to the three stages of Jesus's prayer in Gethsemane.

For a full set of notes on this and other poems, visit www.malachiblack.com.

Acknowledgments

Grateful acknowledgments are made to the editors of the journals in which the following poems first appeared, sometimes in alternate versions:

AGNI: "That the Bones Which Thou Hast Broken May Rejoice"; *AGNI Online:* "Traveling by Train"; *Big Bell:* "Fragments from an Afterlife"; *Blackbird:* "Matins," "Nocturne," "None," and "Sext"; *Boston Review:* "You"; *Columbia: A Journal of Literature and Art:* "Coming & Going"; *Fawlt Magazine:* "Against the Glass" and "Face to Face"; *Glosolalia:* "Morning Shows"; *Gulf Coast:* "As a Draft"; *Harvard Review:* "A Memo to the Self-Possessed"; *Hayden's Ferry Review:* "To the Executioner"; *Indiana Review:* "Awake" and "Growing Season"; *Mid-American Review:* "Metamorphosis"; *Muzzle:* "Plainsong" and "Terce"; *Narrative:* "I Have Forgotten You, My Self" and "Our Lady of Sorrows"; *The New Formalist:* "The Puncture"; *Owen Wister Review:* "Quantum Solstice"; *Passages North:* "Dining after Dawn," "Sleepwalker, Lost," and "Under an Eclipsing Moon"; *Pleiades:* "Compline," "Ode to the Sun," and "Vespers"; *Ploughshares:* "Prayer for a Slow Death" and "When I Lie Down"; *Poetry:* "Drifting at Midday," "Insomnia & So On," "Lauds," "Prime," "Sifting in the Afternoon," and "This Gentle Surgery"; *Southwest Review:* "To the Moon" and "The Winter Traveler"; *32 Poems:* "The Beekeeper's Diary," "Psalm: Pater Noster," and "Query on Typography"; *Washington Square:* "Vigils."

"Whalesong" appeared in *Why Poems Can Be More Like Paintings,* edited by Ana Božičević-Bowling, Caroline

Conway, and Lars Palm (Harmonium Films and Music, 2007). "Traveling by Train" was reprinted in *Best New Poets 2008,* edited by Mark Strand (Samovar Press, 2008). "Dining after Dawn," "Insomnia & So On," "Lauds," "Ode to the Sun," and "Prime" were reprinted in *American Poet: The Journal of the Academy of American Poets.* "To the Executioner" was reprinted on *Verse Daily.* "Found" was printed as a letterpress broadside by Float Press. "Matins," "Sext," and "Vespers" were reprinted in *Poems of Devotion: An Anthology of Recent Poets,* edited by Luke Hankins (Wipf and Stock, 2012). "Vespers" also appears in *Before the Door of God: An Anthology of Devotional Poetry,* edited by Jay Hopler and Kimberly Johnson (Yale University Press, 2013). "Quarantine" was reprinted in whole in *The Poet's Quest for God: 21st Century Poems of Faith, Doubt, and Wonder,* edited by Dr. Oliver Brennan, Todd Swift, and Dominic Bury (Eyewear Publishing [U.K.], 2014). Some of the poems here also appeared in two limited-edition chapbooks: *Echolocation* (Float Press, 2010) and *Quarantine* (Argos Books, 2012).

"Drifting at Midday," "Insomnia & So On," and "You" were set as "Three Songs" by composer Ching-chu Hu and first performed by Brave New Works at Denison University's Tutti New Music Festival in March 2011. "This Gentle Surgery" was rendered as a street art installation by Australia's Melbourne Poetry Project in May 2011. "Drifting at Midday," "Insomnia & So On," "Sifting in the Afternoon," and "This Gentle Surgery" were set to music as the "Black Sonnets" within composer Eric Shanfield's *Very Black Sonnets* opus, published in October 2011. "Prime" was featured in erasure by Michael O. in the "Snow City Arts: Erasures" exhibit, on display at the Poetry Foundation from December 2012–January 2103. "To the Moon," "Mirroring," and "Morning Shows" were set by Ching-chu Hu as "Morning Rearranged," first performed by the Pittsburgh New Music Ensemble at Denison University's Tutti New Music Festival in February 2013.

Special thanks to the generous teachers, friends, readers, editors, and institutions without whom this book would not have been possible: Marla Akin, E.C. Belli, Ana Božičević, the Bread Loaf Writers' Conference, Oliver Brennan, Jericho Brown, Dominic Bury, Tom Cable, Michael Collier, Copper Canyon Press, the Corporation of Yaddo, Tonaya Craft, Steven Dietz, Jonathan Edwards, Nicole Edwards, Emory University, Kelly Forsythe, the Fine Arts Work Center in Provincetown, Dana Gioia, Daniel Grossman, Luke Hankins, Leslie Harrison, Richie Hofmann, Jay Hopler, Marie Howe, Rebecca Gayle Howell, Ching-chu Hu, Ishion Hutchinson, Mark Jarman, Judy Jensen, Kimberly Johnson, Brigit Pegeen Kelly, Caleb Klaces, Yusef Komunyakaa, David Lehman, the MacDowell Colony, Jim Magnuson, Justin Marks, Michael McGriff, Chris Mink, Kristin Naca, Matthew Nienow, Jacqueline Osherow, William Packard, the Poetry Foundation, Matt Rasmussen, Roger Reeves, Paisley Rekdal, Will Schutt, Salvatore Scibona, the Sewanee Writers' Conference, David Shapiro, Jacob Shores-Argüello, Ed Skoog, Eric Smith, Bruce Snider, A.E. Stallings, Mark Strand, Todd Swift, Chris Tonelli, Natasha Trethewey, the University of Texas at Austin's Michener Center for Writers, the University of Utah's Department of English, the West Chester University Poetry Conference, Marcus Wicker, Michael Wiegers, and Matthew Yeager. Emphatic, everlasting gratitude to Dean Young and Laurie Saurborn Young for invaluable friendship, guidance, and support. Enduring love to my family and to Carmen Radley, for all she is and does.

About the Author

Malachi Black was born in Boston, Massachusetts, and raised in Morris County, New Jersey. He holds a B.A. from New York University, an M.F.A. from the University of Texas at Austin's Michener Center for Writers, and a Ph.D. in Literature with Creative Writing from the University of Utah. The recipient of a 2009 Ruth Lilly Fellowship (awarded by the Poetry Foundation in conjunction with *Poetry* magazine), Black has since received fellowships and awards from the Bread Loaf Writers' Conference, the Corporation of Yaddo, Emory University, the Fine Arts Work Center in Provincetown, the MacDowell Colony, and the Sewanee Writers' Conference. His poems appear widely in journals and anthologies, and his work has several times been set to music and has been featured in exhibitions both in the U.S. and abroad. Black is Assistant Professor of English and Creative Writing at the University of San Diego.

Lannan Literary Selections

For two decades Lannan Foundation has supported the publication and distribution of exceptional literary works. Copper Canyon Press gratefully acknowledges their support.

LANNAN LITERARY SELECTIONS 2014

Mark Bibbins, *They Don't Kill You Because They're Hungry, They Kill You Because They're Full*

Malachi Black, *Storm Toward Morning*

Marianne Boruch, *Cadaver, Speak*

Jericho Brown, *The New Testament*

Olena Kalytiak Davis, *The Poem She Didn't Write and Other Poems*

RECENT LANNAN LITERARY SELECTIONS FROM COPPER CANYON PRESS

James Arthur, *Charms Against Lightning*

Natalie Diaz, *When My Brother Was an Aztec*

Matthew Dickman and Michael Dickman, *50 American Plays*

Michael Dickman, *Flies*

Kerry James Evans, *Bangalore*

Tung-Hui Hu, *Greenhouses, Lighthouses*

Laura Kasischke, *Space, in Chains*

Deborah Landau, *The Last Usable Hour*

Sarah Lindsay, *Debt to the Bone-Eating Snotflower*

Michael McGriff, *Home Burial*

Valzhyna Mort, *Collected Body*

Lisa Olstein, *Little Stranger*

Roger Reeves, *King Me*

Ed Skoog, *Rough Day*

John Taggart, *Is Music: Selected Poems*

Jean Valentine, *Break the Glass*

Dean Young, *Fall Higher*

For a complete list of Lannan Literary Selections from Copper Canyon Press, please visit Partners on our website: www.coppercanyonpress.org

Poetry is vital to language and living. Since 1972, Copper Canyon Press has published extraordinary poetry from around the world to engage the imaginations and intellects of readers, writers, booksellers, librarians, teachers, students, and donors.

WE ARE GRATEFUL FOR THE MAJOR SUPPORT PROVIDED BY:

THE PAUL G. ALLEN
FAMILY FOUNDATION

THE MAURER FAMILY
FOUNDATION

ART WORKS. | National Endowment for the Arts
arts.gov

A&
OFFICE OF ARTS & CULTURE
SEATTLE

WASHINGTON STATE
ARTS COMMISSION

Anonymous

John Branch

Diana Broze

Beroz Ferrell & The Point, LLC

Janet and Les Cox

Mimi Gardner Gates

Gull Industries, Inc.
on behalf of William and Ruth True

Linda Gerrard and Walter Parsons

Mark Hamilton and Suzie Rapp

Carolyn and Robert Hedin

Steven Myron Holl

Lakeside Industries, Inc.
on behalf of Jeanne Marie Lee

Maureen Lee and Mark Busto

Brice Marden

Ellie Mathews and Carl Youngmann as
The North Press

H. Stewart Parker

Penny and Jerry Peabody

John Phillips and Anne O'Donnell

Joseph C. Roberts

Cynthia Lovelace Sears and Frank Buxton

The Seattle Foundation

Dan Waggoner

Charles and Barbara Wright

The dedicated interns and faithful volunteers of Copper Canyon Press

TO LEARN MORE ABOUT UNDERWRITING COPPER CANYON PRESS TITLES,
PLEASE CALL 360-385-4925 EXT. 103

The Chinese character for poetry is made up of two parts:
"word" and "temple." It also serves as pressmark for
Copper Canyon Press.

The poems are set in Sabon.
Book design and composition by Phil Kovacevich.